BookLife PUBLISHING

©2023
BookLife Publishing Ltd.
King's Lynn, Norfolk
PE30 4LS, UK

All rights reserved.
Printed in China.

A catalogue record for this book is available from the British Library.

ISBN: 978-1-80505-026-1

Written by:
Charis Mather
Adapted by:
Noah Leatherland
Edited by:
Rod Barkman
Designed by:
Amy Li

All facts, statistics, web addresses and URLs in this book were verified as valid and accurate at time of writing. No responsibility for any changes to external websites or references can be accepted by either the author or publisher.

AN INTRODUCTION TO BOOKLIFE RAPID READERS...

Packed full of gripping topics and twisted tales, BookLife Rapid Readers are perfect for older children looking to propel their reading up to top speed. With three levels based on our planet's fastest animals, children will be able to find the perfect point from which to accelerate their reading journey. From the spooky to the silly, these roaring reads will turn every child at every reading level into a prolific page-turner!

CHEETAH
The fastest animals on land, cheetahs will be taking their first strides as they race to top speed.

MARLIN
The fastest animals under water, marlins will be blasting through their journey.

FALCON
The fastest animals in the air, falcons will be flying at top speed as they tear through the skies.

Photo Credits – Images are courtesy of Shutterstock.com. With thanks to Getty Images, Thinkstock Photo and iStockphoto. Recurring images – Marina Santiaga, aopsan, Gaidamashchuk, DLA. Cover – MagicPics, Redcollegiya, Seahorse Vector. 4–5 – T Studio, Tithi Luadthong. 6–7 – Design Projects. 8–9 – Panaiotidi, DM7, tsuneomp. 10–11 – adike, yas1nshah. 12–13 – BLACKDAY, Melkor3D. 14–15 – Design Projects, ShotbyDSN. 16–17 – Tithi Luadthong, Liu zishan. 18–19 – insima, Tanya Syrytsyna. 20–21 – Erni, Vadim Zakharishchev. 22–23 – crbellette, Silmiart. 24–25 – IG Digital Arts, Joeprachatree. 26–27 – Anna Vasiljeva, delcarmat. 28–29 – e71lena, Melkor3D. 30 – KK Tan.

CONTENTS

PAGE 4   The Mystery of the Dragon
PAGE 6   Dragon Spotter's Guide
PAGE 8   Flying High
PAGE 10   Dragon Magic
PAGE 14   Everything We Know
PAGE 18   Different Dragons
PAGE 20   Easy Mistake to Make...
PAGE 24   Impostor!
PAGE 28   Hidden Hideouts
PAGE 30   Creatures of Myth
PAGE 31   Glossary
PAGE 32   Index

Words that look like this are explained in the glossary on page 31.

THE MYSTERY OF THE DRAGON

You have probably heard of dragons, but have you ever seen one before? Dragons are mythical creatures. Mythical creatures are beings found in old stories and <u>legends</u>.

There are lots of stories about dragons, but no one is sure if they ever really existed. As far as we know, there are no creatures now on Earth like the dragons from the legends.

People have been telling stories of dragons for thousands of years. The stories talk about their great power and the brave people that went looking for them.

All these stories make you wonder... could dragons really have existed once? Could there still be a few dragons hidden around the world?

DRAGON
SPOTTER'S GUIDE

If you ever spot something that you think might be a dragon, look out for these things:

LARGE WINGS
Dragon wings are tough and leathery. They have wings like a bat.

LONG TAIL
Dragon tails help them to fly by keeping them balanced.

TOUGH SCALES
<u>Scales</u> protect the dragon like a shield and let them move freely.

SHARP TEETH
A dragon uses its teeth for hunting and protecting itself.

LONG NECK

SHARP CLAWS

FLYING HIGH

Creatures as big as dragons do not normally fly. However, dragons have a few tricks that help them soar through the air.

LARGE WINGS

A dragon's wings can stretch out really wide. When they flap their wings, they push huge amounts of air to lift the dragon off the ground.

HOLLOW BONES

A creature the size of a dragon clearly needs very large, strong bones. Dragon bones are also like a bird's bones. Birds have bones that are <u>hollow</u>, which makes them much lighter.

Dragons have hollow bones just like this to help them take flight. There is also something else that helps dragons fly... MAGIC!

DRAGON MAGIC

As well as being able to fly, dragons are known for being very powerful. Dragons are best known for being able to breathe fire. Some people think that dragons have a liquid stored in their bodies that sets on fire when it is sprayed from their mouths.

Or maybe it is just magic!

Spraying fire out of their mouths could be very painful for most animals. Dragons are not bothered by the heat. Their mouths are fireproof to stop them from getting burnt.

A dragon's scales are also fireproof. This stops them from hurting themselves when they are breathing fire.

Other stories say that different dragons can have different types of breath. People have told stories about dragons that breathe ice, some that breathe acid and some that breathe lightning.

Some stories say that dragons can shapeshift. This means that they can change their shape and what they look like. These stories say that dragons sometimes change into humans so that they can hide without being bothered.

Perhaps you have seen someone you might think is secretly a dragon?

EVERYTHING WE KNOW

It is hard to tell exactly how long dragons live for. They live much longer than humans, which is why people have found it hard to keep track of a dragon's age.

Some stories say that dragons live for about 100 years. Others say that they can live for around 10,000 years. Some legends say that dragons can live forever!

Dragons hatch from small, shiny eggs. Baby dragons are tiny, so they need to eat a lot of food to become full-sized.

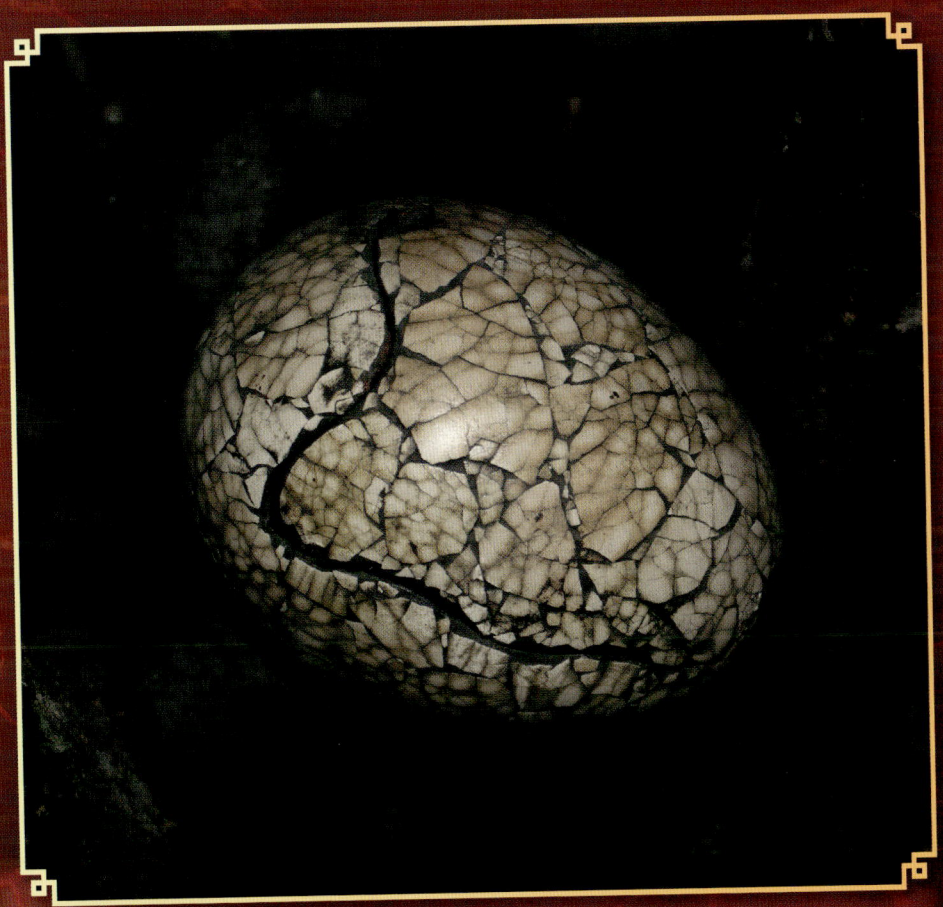

Dragons are meat-eaters. They get their food from hunting and eating animals. Be careful if you go looking for dragons because they sometimes eat humans, too!

Dragons are much smarter than most creatures. They are not just mindless killers like some other mythical creatures. Some legends talk about dragons that are even smarter than humans!

A fight with a dragon is already hard to win because of their beastly teeth, claws and fire breath. However, a dragon's <u>intelligence</u> makes a battle with them even more difficult.

Some stories say that some dragons can even speak! They say that dragons have their own language to speak to each other, but dragons can also speak to humans.

Stories about talking dragons say that they love to give people <u>riddles</u>. They might give you a riddle just for fun… or under the threat of eating you!

DIFFERENT DRAGONS

Dragons that have wings and can breathe fire are sometimes known as Western dragons. These are the most famous dragons, but there are lots of different types in other legends.

In most parts of Asia, there are stories of dragons without wings that can not breathe fire. People believe that Eastern dragons fly by the power of magic alone.

Eastern dragons come in lots of different colours. Rather than breathing fire, Eastern dragons have the power to control water, including rain and clouds.

Eastern dragons are long, thin creatures, almost like giant snakes. Their scales are not as strong as Western dragon scales. Instead, they are more like fish scales to help them move.

EASY MISTAKE
TO MAKE...

As far as we know, there are no animals in the real world that breathe fire. However, there are a few animals that do make good dragon <u>impostors</u>.

BEARDED DRAGON

Lizards are probably the closest thing we have found to the mythical dragons from the stories. Some lizards even have the word dragon in their name.

KOMODO DRAGONS

While nowhere near as big as the mythical dragons, Komodo dragons are still an impressive size. In fact, they are the largest lizards in the world.

Komodo dragons do not have wings to fly, but they do have sharp claws and teeth. They do not breathe fire, but they do have <u>venom</u> in their spit that helps them hunt.

DRACO LIZARDS

Draco lizards are sometimes called flying dragon lizards. They have flaps of skin that they use to <u>glide</u> between trees in the rainforests and jungles they live in. This is not quite flying, but it is pretty close.

There are over 40 types of draco lizard. On average, they are about 20 centimetres long, and half of that is their tails.

THORNY DEVILS

The thorny devil is a lizard sometimes called the thorny dragon. Its entire body is covered in spikes to protect it from <u>predators</u>. It also has a 'false head' to confuse predators.

Thorny devils live in sandy parts of Australia. They have special scales that help them drink water by touching it with any part of their body.

IMPOSTOR!

Dragon impostors are found in the world of mythical creatures, too!

HYDRAS

Hydras are large beasts with many heads that look like snakes. The stories say that one of their heads can breathe fire, just like a dragon.

In the legends, hydras are very hard to beat. That is because it is said that cutting off a hydra's head does not kill it... It just makes it grow more heads!

WYVERNS

Wyverns look a lot like dragons. While most dragons are shown with four legs, wyverns are only shown with two. The legends say that wyverns are smaller and not as intelligent as dragons.

It is not clear if wyverns can breathe fire or not. Some wyverns are said to have venomous stingers on their tails. They are very dangerous creatures.

LINDWORMS

Lindworms can also be confused with dragons. They are giant mythical snakes that sometimes have parts that look like a dragon.

Some stories say lindworms have wings, and other stories say that lindworms have claws on their snake bodies. Even if they have do wings, lindworms slither everywhere.

BASILISKS

A basilisk is another creature that has a lot of features like a dragon. It has wings and a body like a lizard but the head of a rooster.

Instead of breathing fire or using sharp claws, stories of the basilisk say it can turn people and other creatures into stone just by looking at them.

HIDDEN HIDEOUTS

The best spots to look for dragons are far away from places where lots of people live. Dragons do not like to be disturbed. They make their lairs far away from humans to find peace.

The legends of dragons talk about some places to find them. Dragons like high mountains with large caves. They also like taking over old, empty castles.

It might take a long time to find a dragon's hiding place. What is hidden inside might make it worth it, though. Legends say that dragons spend their lives collecting treasure to keep in their lairs.

Beware, though. Dragons do not like people coming for their gold. They will attack anyone who tries to take even a single coin from their treasure.

CREATURES
OF MYTH

Dragons are mysterious creatures. We can never quite be sure if the stories about them are true. We can only sit and wonder what they might be like.

The best way to keep learning about dragons is to keep reading. There are so many stories and legends about dragons from all over the world. Who knows what you might learn?

GLOSSARY

GLIDE	to move in a smooth motion without flapping
HOLLOW	empty on the inside
IMPOSTORS	things that pretend to be something else
INTELLIGENCE	the ability to learn or understand things
LEGENDS	stories from the past that may have a mix of truth and made-up things
LIQUID	a material that flows, such as water
PREDATORS	animals that hunt other animals for food
RIDDLES	tricky questions that are asked as a puzzle to solve
SCALES	small, overlapping flakes, as found on animals such as fish and snakes
VENOM	a poison that is injected by a bite or sting

INDEX

BASILISKS 27

BONES 9

FIRE 10–11, 16, 18–21, 24–25, 27

HYDRAS 24

IMPOSTORS 20, 24

KOMODO DRAGONS 21

LINDWORMS 26

LIZARDS 20–23, 27

TREASURE 29

WYVERNS 25